DON'T TOUCH THAT!

The BOOK of GROSS, POISONOUS, and DOWNright ICKY Plants and critters

Jeff Day, M.D.

CHICAGO

Library of Congress Cataloging-in-Publication Data

Day, Jeff, 1980–

Don't touch that : the book of gross, poisonous, and downright icky plants and critters / Jeff Day.

p. cm.

Includes index.

ISBN-13: 978-1-55652-711-1

ISBN-10: 1-55652-711-X

1. Poisons—Safety measures—Juvenile literature. 2. Poisons—Treatment—Juvenile literature. 3. Poisonous animals—Juvenile literature. 4. Poisonous plants—Juvenile literature. I. Title.

RA1214.D39 2006

363.17′91—dc22   2007027466

The information in this book is provided for educational and informational purposes only and is not intended to be a substitute for a health care provider's consultation.

Cover and interior design: Monica Baziuk
Cover and interior illustrations: Jeff Day

Published by Chicago Review Press, Incorporated
814 North Franklin Street
Chicago, Illinois 60610
ISBN: 978-1-55652-711-1
Printed in China

5 4 3 2 1

Contents

Has This Ever
Happened
to You? — 1

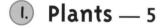

Thanks to Martin Rosenberg, Ph.D.,

Joe Keiper, Ph.D., and Tom Volk, Ph.D.

for answering my queries and inspiring exploration.

Thanks for the support of the

Primary Care Track family at the Case Western Reserve

University School of Medicine.

Of course, biggest thanks

go to Mom and Dad—love always.

Has This Ever Happened to You?

You see a strange blob on the ground.

You stoop down to get a closer look.

Maybe a thought flashes across your brain subconsciously . . .

Don't touch that! It could be poisonous!

or maybe a friend standing next to you barks those lines like a frantic seal.

Either way, you get the warning.

Nature is waiting for you to explore all its wonders. This book will help you learn about some of the most common and most dangerous things that are *not* safe to touch. You also will learn proper first aid for dangerous scenarios. And hopefully, you will walk away eager to learn more and ready to conquer the mysteries of the wilderness.

I'm waiting...?

Mother Nature

This book is *not* titled *Don't Eat That!* While there actually are many delicacies to be found in the great outdoors, some things are far too dangerous to put in your mouth. Many edible and not-so-edible things can easily be confused with each other. This book does not recommend eating anything you find outside, unless you are with someone who really knows what he or she is doing! Touching is OK. Eating is *not* OK.

Wait! Stop! That's a **poison** cheeseburger tree!

Much of this book deals with poison and venom, both of which are chemical substances that can cause immediate danger or pain. *Venom* is injected, usually by the bite or sting of an animal, such as a snake or a spider.

Venom

Poison is a substance that is harmful when you touch or swallow it, such as the skin of a poison dart frog.

Poison

Plants 1

Poison Ivy

How many times has someone told you, "Don't touch that! It could be poison ivy!"? Well, now you can know the *truth* about poison ivy!

Who Gets Poison Ivy?

Me?

Yeah, that's right: you!

(Not you.)

Poison ivy is the #1 most common "poisonous" plant that affects humans in the United States.

Oddly enough, only humans and some other primates—monkeys and apes—get itchy when they touch poison ivy.

Boy, I sure am glad poison ivy doesn't grow in Borneo!

Boy, I sure am glad orangutans **do** grow in Borneo!

Other animals can touch the stuff all the time and nothing will happen. Many animals even enjoy *eating* poison ivy!

One Leaf, Three Leaflets

So how can you tell what poison ivy looks like? There's a handy phrase: "Leaves of three, leave it be." That's a good rule of thumb. Actually, more accurately, the phrase should say, *"Leaflets* of three." Each poison ivy leaf is composed of three leaflets. All three leaflets share one stem. Together they form one leaf.

Poison ivy leaf

Three leaflets

Leaves can grow many different ways. Some are called simple leaves and others are called compound leaves. *Simple leaves* are attached directly to branches.

Compound leaves are leaves composed of leaflets. Leaflets look like leaves, but they combine to form one big leaf. Leaflets are attached to stems that are usually green and soft, just like the stems on simple leaves. These green stems are different from branches, which are hard and woody. You will see a nice, clean scar on a branch where a whole leaf has been plucked off, for either a compound or a simple leaf.

Poison ivy leaves are compound leaves, which means they have several leaflets per leaf.

Compound leaf

Simple leaf

Branch

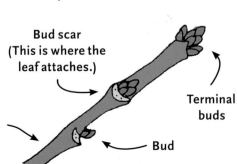

Bud scar
(This is where the leaf attaches.)

Twig

Terminal buds

Bud

This is a compound leaf shaped like a hand. Buckeye and horse chestnut trees have these types of compound leaves.

Leaf

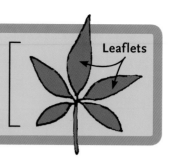

Leaflets

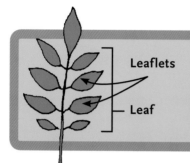

Leaflets

Leaf

This is a compound leaf shaped like a pin. Ashes, walnuts, hickories, and locusts have these types of compound leaves.

Looking at Leaves

Here are some simple leaf shapes. Can you find any of these leaf shapes and features on the plants outside?

This leaf is shaped like an oval. Its edges are smooth. Poison ivy leaflets have this shape and have mostly smooth edges.

This leaf has teeth along the edges.

This leaf has big gaps along its edges. The gaps are called *sinuses,* and the parts that stick out are called *lobes.* Poison ivy leaflets may have some tooth-like lobes.

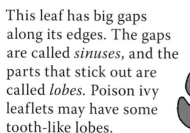

This leaf is shaped like a heart.

This leaf is shaped like a hand. It also has lobes and sinuses.

This leaf is shaped like Abe Lincoln. Not too common.

The Many Faces of Poison Ivy

Poison ivy can be tough to identify because it can grow as a vine on a tree, as a little plant on the ground, or even as a shrub.

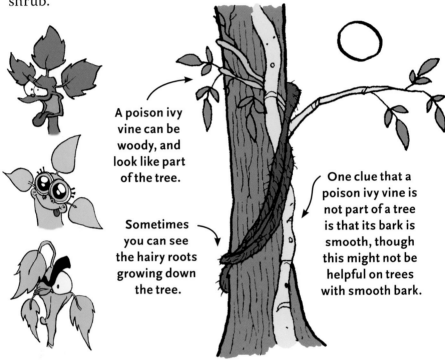

A poison ivy vine can be woody, and look like part of the tree.

Sometimes you can see the hairy roots growing down the tree.

One clue that a poison ivy vine is not part of a tree is that its bark is smooth, though this might not be helpful on trees with smooth bark.

Some harmless plants may look like poison ivy growing on the tree. However, if you're not sure, just play it safe!

What is that funny circle floating next to the tree? The sun? The moon? Nope, just a sketch from a lazy artist. It's supposed to be a close-up view of a poison ivy berry. This berry is special because it is white. Have you ever seen a white berry? At the grocery store, you can buy berries that are red or blue or black, but the store never sells white ones. A white berry is a good indication that the plant it comes from might be poisonous. Poison ivy, poison sumac, and poison oak all have white berries.

Poison Oak and Poison Sumac

Poison oak and poison sumac give people reactions very similar to the one you get from poison ivy, but poison ivy, the most common of the three, is still the king of rashes!

Like poison ivy, poison oak and poison sumac secrete the same oil that makes us itchy. Poison ivy can be found throughout most of the continental United States. Poison oak is also found throughout the United States, but is more common in the West. Poison sumac is found in the East, mostly in the southeastern United States.

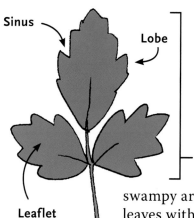

Sinus

Lobe

Leaf

Leaflet

Poison oak leaves look like poison ivy leaves, but they have more wavy edges, called lobes and sinuses.

Poison oak leaf

Poison sumac is a small shrub that grows around swampy areas. Poison sumac has compound leaves with more than three leaflets. Often the middle stem that all the leaflets grow on is reddish in color.

Poison sumac

The leaves of these plants can look a lot like the leaves of many other safe plants. However, if you are not in a swamp, you probably are not looking at a poison sumac. If you are not sure and want to play it safe, just remember: "Leaves of three, leave it be."

Itchy, Itchy Oil

The part of poison ivy that makes people itch is the oil that grows inside the plant. The oil comes out of the plant only when the plant is broken or injured. You can actually touch poison ivy without getting the itch, as long as you do not touch the oil.

Poison ivy oil is clear, but when it touches oxygen, it turns black. Some Native Americans even used the black oil as a dye.

But not hair dye!

Sometimes you can still see the old black oil on the stems of poison ivy in the wintertime, after the leaves have fallen off. Leftover oil can make you itch even years after it oozed out of the plant, so if you think it is poison ivy, don't touch it!

Actually, you should not touch *any* part of poison ivy. There may be tiny breaks in the plant that you cannot see where oil has come out. It only takes a little bit of oil to give you a large bit of itching!

An inappropriate touching of poison ivy.

So why does poison ivy even make the oil? Just to drive humans crazy? Actually, the oil helps protect the plant when it gets hurt. It oozes out and seals the injury like glue. In other words, poison ivy makes its own Band-Aids! Humans are just unlucky that they are allergic to the oil.

Somebody call an ambulance! I'm wounded!

You may have heard that burning poison ivy can give people itchy reactions. This is *true*! Oil particles can be carried with the dust and ashes that float through the air, and those particles might get on your skin if you are standing in the area.

The Rash

What happens in a reaction to poison ivy oil? Luckily, we have a brave (and very itchy) teddy bear volunteer to demonstrate.

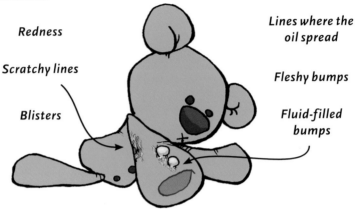

Redness

Scratchy lines

Blisters

Lines where the oil spread

Fleshy bumps

Fluid-filled bumps

Depending on the severity of the reaction, poison ivy rashes can take different lengths of time to heal. On average, they take about two weeks to completely heal.

Is poison ivy contagious? Nope. After you wash the poison ivy oil from your skin, you can't transfer it to other people. Some people get little blisters that may weep fluid, but touching this fluid will not give you a poison ivy rash. The fluid in the blisters is part of the allergic reaction and is different from the poison ivy oil.

Poison ivy is a type of *contact dermatitis*—basically a rash from touching stuff. Some people cannot touch latex (rubber) gloves. Some people cannot touch nickel, which is used to make belt buckles and watches, in addition to five-cent coins. Poison ivy is one of the most common things that can give you a rash when you touch it.

Teddy bear has a nickel allergy rash from his belt buckle.

Contact dermatitis is a type of allergy. For more on how allergies work, see *Anaphylaxis* on page 36. Contact dermatitis is a different type of allergy than the type of allergy people get from bee stings or eating peanuts. Contact dermatitis does not give you anaphylaxis, but it sure can be uncomfortable!

Like other types of allergies, people first have to be sensitized to whatever they are allergic to. That is, their bodies have to "see" the allergen at least once before becoming allergic to it. In the case of poison ivy, the first time your body touches the plant, maybe nothing will happen. Nothing will happen until the second time, or maybe even the hundredth time you touch the plant. The more you touch the plant, the more likely it is that you may develop an allergic reaction in the future.

Not everyone gets itchy when they touch poison ivy though. Some experts guess that about seven out of ten people are sensitive to poison ivy.

Contact dermatitis, a type of allergy.

Weird, supernatural chemical reaction.

What Should I Do If I Get Poison Ivy?

The best thing to do is not to touch poison ivy in the first place. PREVENTION! Learn what poison ivy looks like, and avoid it. If you are hiking in the woods, you also might want to wear long pants and a long shirt.

But if you *do* touch poison ivy, follow these steps.

I spread the oil around with my Batman stencil. **Batman rash!**

STEP 1   **Do not scratch or touch the area where you touched the plant.**

Scratching spreads the oil, which can give you more rashes.

STEP 2   **Wash the area with soap and cold water.**

If you think you have touched poison ivy, it is important to wash your hands and clothes with soap as soon as possible. Soap breaks down the poison ivy oils. If you wash off the oils quickly enough (within a few hours of touching the plant), it is possible that you will not have a reaction. Washing also helps to prevent you from spreading the oil to other parts of your body or to other people. Using cold water helps to keep your pores closed so that less oil can get into them. After you have washed, it is safe to touch all areas of your body.

STEP 3   **Use stuff for comfort as needed, like calamine lotion.**

Some people find comfort in an oatmeal bath. Calamine lotion can be quite soothing. Calamine lotion is also much easier than oatmeal bathing.

Oatmeal baths might help you feel better, but Fruit Loops do not work.

I wish I got to bathe in Fruit Loops.

STEP 4 See a doctor if your rash is really bad, or if you have questions.

A doctor might be able to give you a little something extra if you get it bad.

Jewelweed

Touch me not—I'm about to blow!

Jewelweed is a popular folk treatment for poison ivy. This plant can be found growing outside, sometimes (conveniently) next to poison ivy plants. It is sometimes called a "spotted touch-me-not" because if you touch the seedpod the right way, it explodes! Don't worry, it won't hurt you.

Jewelweed seed pod

Jewelweed is easy to recognize because of its unique orange or yellow flowers. People rub the juices from the stem on skin that has touched the poison ivy. Though it is not scientifically proven to help, it probably doesn't hurt—plus it's a cool plant to find!

Jewelweed

Other Plants to Watch Out For

Many other plants can cause skin problems, but in North America the most common is poison ivy. Here are a few more plants that you should watch out for.

Thorny Plants

Some plants have thorns, so it is pretty obvious that they could hurt you. Sometimes plants may have tiny thorns, or even hairs that are difficult to see, and these plants can

Cactus diving: not recommended.

cause rashes in a sensitive person. Unlike poison ivy oil, these thorns or hairs are actually meant to protect the plant from hungry animals. Some plants that grow in the United States and have these tiny hairs or thorns are thistles, prickly pears, tulip bulbs, and some grasses.

Trumpet Creeper

Also called cow itch vine, this plant is commonly planted in yards. It has pretty, trumpet-like flowers. Its leaves and flowers may cause an itchy reaction. Not everyone is affected—it is just one of many plants that can give people an itchy reaction.

Some plants secrete milky sap when they are injured. This sap may cause irritating rashes in some people. Examples include milkweed and euphorbs, which are common cactuslike houseplants.

Giant Hogweed

This giant plant was introduced into American gardens from Europe. It produces a clear sap that causes *photodermatitis,* which means the skin it touches is extra sensitive to the sun and gets burned easily, causing rashes and blisters.

Stinging Nettle

One plant that is particularly painful to touch is the stinging nettle. It is kind of hard to identify by sight. The easiest way to identify it is to walk into it—and feel its stinging wrath!

Stinging nettles have lots of tiny hairs that stick to our bodies and release chemicals that sting and itch. Washing with cool water is always a good idea, but mixing baking soda into the water may provide more relief. Jewelweed has also been said to help (see page 17). If you run into stinging nettle, try not to scratch, because that can make the stinging worse. The stinging can be quite painful and may last anywhere from an hour to a day.

Stinging nettle is found throughout most of North America. Interestingly, the leaves of stinging nettle can actually be eaten (when cooked) or made into tea!

Carnivorous Plants

Yes, plants that eat animals really do exist!

Venus Flytrap

The most famous carnivorous plant is the Venus flytrap because of its mouthlike leaves. Sorry to disappoint you, but they do not eat people. However, what if you stuck your finger in one? Would that be dangerous?

Not likely. You are much stronger than a Venus flytrap and could easily pull your finger back out. When the plant eats a bug, digestion usually takes about ten days. You probably wouldn't sit with your finger being digested in a plant for ten days.

This Venus flytrap illustration might be more accurate if cows were only one inch long. Venus flytraps are not very big.

Unfortunately, Venus flytraps are becoming rare, and they only grow in North and South Carolina. They grow in wet, boggy soil that does not have many nutrients and make up for it by eating insects. The plants secrete nectar and have special coloring to attract insects. Hairs on the plant can sense when an insect enters, triggering a superfast closure of the plant lids.

There were once myths of giant man-eating plants, but the Venus flytrap is actually quite small. Like most plants, it gets most of its energy from the sun. In a lifetime, these plants may only catch three or four insects.

Venus flytraps are the fastest moving plant. When you think of a plant, you might imagine a boring green thing that sits still, but plants actually *do* move. Some plants will move toward sunlight, and their roots can "feel" gravity, growing downward rather than from side to side. Some plants will curl up when touched, some have tendrils that look for things to grab onto, and some have exploding seedpods. Plants may not be able to run or jump, but they are a lot more active than you might think.

Venus flytraps are the fastest plants.

People can keep Venus flytraps as "pets." But they shouldn't share their food with the plant because humans' high-fat meats can actually rot the plant. They should only be fed insects and water.

Pitcher Plants and More

There are other plants that also feed on insects, such as pitcher plants and bladderworts. These plants, like the Venus flytrap, grow in environments that are not rich in nutrients.

Where's the lifeguard?!

Pitcher plants are carnivorous plants that attract insects and drown them.

Fungi

What is a fungus? Some people think fungi (the plural of fungus) are kind of like plants. One big difference is that plants can produce their own food from the sun, whereas fungi need to "eat" things. Fungi are very important for helping to decompose things, or break them down. Fungi help turn dead plants and animals into the soil on the ground.

These mushrooms are turning the dead log into soil.

Mushrooms are probably the most famous fungi, but other examples of fungi include molds and yeasts. Some fungi can cause diseases like ringworm or athlete's foot.

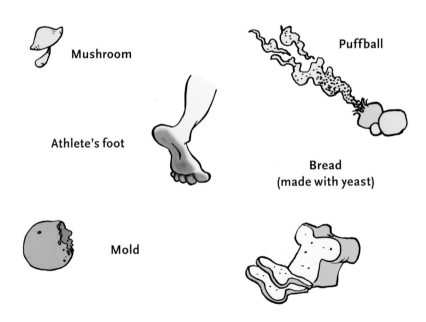

Mushroom

Puffball

Athlete's foot

Bread
(made with yeast)

Mold

What is a mushroom? A mushroom is a fruiting body of a larger organism. Most of a mushroom fungus grows underground and looks like threads or hairs. When the time is right, a mushroom—the fruiting body—will pop up out of the ground. The fruiting body releases spores so that new mushrooms can grow in other places.

Can you find these parts on a wild mushroom?

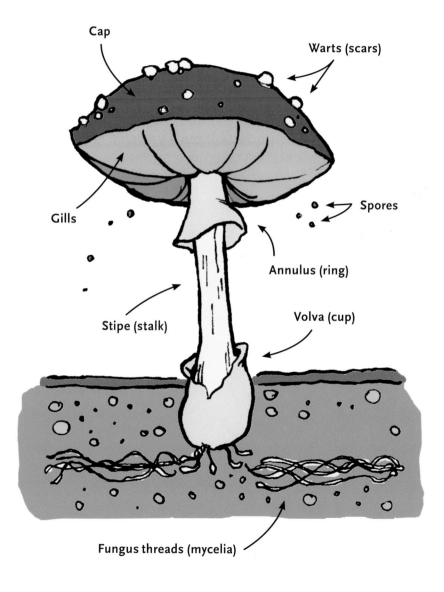

Cap

Warts (scars)

Spores

Gills

Annulus (ring)

Stipe (stalk)

Volva (cup)

Fungus threads (mycelia)

Some mushrooms are super poisonous—so poisonous that you could die if you ate enough of them. Other mushrooms may not kill you, but they could make you very sick. Of course, store-bought mushrooms are all safe to eat.

Because mushrooms are pretty hard to tell apart, you should *never* try tasting any wild mushroom by yourself. For the most part, mushrooms are safe to touch, even the most dangerous ones such as the "destroying angel." But always remember: **NEVER EAT WILD MUSHROOMS!**

Interestingly, rabbits can eat the deadly destroying angel mushroom without any harm. Note to yourself: don't let a rabbit make you a mushroom pizza!

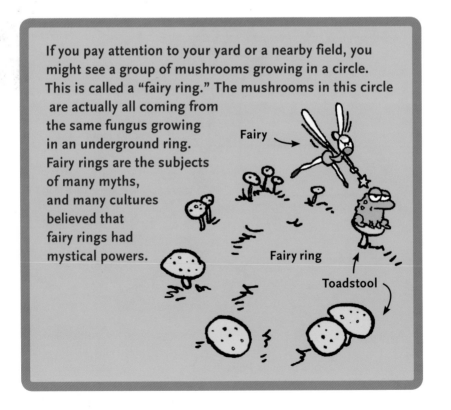

If you pay attention to your yard or a nearby field, you might see a group of mushrooms growing in a circle. This is called a "fairy ring." The mushrooms in this circle are actually all coming from the same fungus growing in an underground ring. Fairy rings are the subjects of many myths, and many cultures believed that fairy rings had mystical powers.

Fairy

Fairy ring

Toadstool

Insects 2

Arthropods (Bugs)

Arthropods are commonly referred to as "bugs." This group encompasses a wide range of animals, some of which include:

Insects have six legs and three body segments. They include ants, butterflies, beetles, grasshoppers, and much more.

Centipedes and Millipedes have lots of body segments and lots of legs.

Crustaceans have hard exoskeletons. They include crabs and lobsters.

Arachnids have eight legs and two body segments. They include spiders, scorpions, and ticks.

Bugs: What's in a Name?

When people say the word "bug," they are usually talking about anything that is a creepy crawly. However, scientists use the term bug for a specific group of insects. True bugs have strawlike mouths for sucking, and two pairs of flat

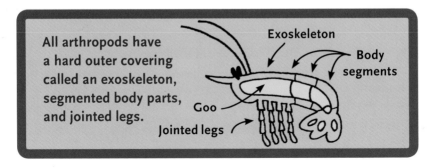

All arthropods have a hard outer covering called an exoskeleton, segmented body parts, and jointed legs.

Exoskeleton

Body segments

Goo

Jointed legs

wings behind a triangular shield on their backs. Instead of the word "bug," this book will say "buggeroos" when referring to creepy crawlies.

Here are several types of *true* bugs:

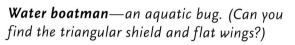

Wheel Bug—*these critters bite! (Notice the slurpy strawmouth.)*

Water boatman—*an aquatic bug. (Can you find the triangular shield and flat wings?)*

Stinkbug—*it's stinky when crushed.*

Ladybug—*FAKE OUT! Ladybugs are actually types of beetles, not bugs. They have mouths that chew rather than suck, and they have a pair of hard, thick wings on their backs that true bugs don't have.*

Biting Buggeroos

Many buggeroos bite, including mosquitoes, biting flies, true bugs, and fleas. Usually these bites only result in itchy bumps or mild pain. Occasionally, some of these little guys can spread disease, especially the mosquitoes. In this section, you will read about bites and stings that may be a little more worrisome to people.

A lot of people are creeped out by arthropods. Maybe it's because some of them bite, some of them spread disease, and all of them look like alien monsters under the microscope. However, these little animals are very important in the environment.

Bees and Wasps

The guy on the right is about to bash this bee-home to smithereens. Good idea or bad idea? BAD IDEA! You don't need to be a fortune teller to know that pain is in his future.

But wait! Although you know the guy here is in for a world of hurt, do you know what dangerous critters actually live in that "bee-home"? Bees? Wasps? Fairies with really sharp teeth? You can see the answer below.*

There are many insects that people commonly call "bees" or "wasps." Some of them sting and some of them don't. In general, bees are nicer and wasps are more likely to sting. There are also wasps that do not sting. And even more confusing, there are some harmless insects that just try to look like bees and wasps for protection.

Bees and wasps have sharply contrasting black and yellow stripes. This is just like human caution tape, which screams "Danger!"

CAUTION GIANT WASP

Some harmless insects like this hoverfly pretend to be dangerous by sporting caution-tape colors.

*The hairy man above is happily swatting a paper wasp nest. He won't be happy for long!

Only female bees and wasps sting. The stinger is an adaptation of the ovipositor, an insect's egg-laying structure, and only females lay eggs.

So if bees are nicer than wasps, what are some ways to tell them apart? Here are a few simple methods:

1. Bees are much hairier than wasps. The hair helps them carry pollen from flower to flower, and static electricity on the fuzz helps the pollen stick.

2. The two long back legs of a wasp dangle down as it flies around. Bees are a lot stockier.

3. Color is usually a bad identification clue. However, honeybees typically have a tan-orange color while stinging wasps and hornets have more sharply contrasting bright yellows and blacks.

4. Wasps have large jaws for attacking insects, but bees have straws for sucking nectar.

Wasp

5. Bees hang out around flowers, sucking nectar. Wasps do not really stop at flowers.

6. Bees build waxy *honeycomb* hives in crevices found in trees, house walls, or man-made beehives. Wasps, on the other hand, build gray, *papery* nests. Wasp nests can hang by themselves or be found in crevices. Harming a nest or hive is the best way to get stung, regardless of whether a bee or wasp made it.

Bee

Bees

The insect family *Apidae* includes honeybees and bumblebees. These insects are generally nicer than insects in the wasp family, *Vespidae.* Although bees can sting, they usually only do it when provoked, such as when dudes swing at them with baseball bats. Sheesh—who would do that?

Bumblebee

Honeybee

Honeybees are unique because their stingers have barbs that get stuck in their victims. When the bees pull away, their stingers stay stuck, along with some important body parts necessary for survival. That's why honeybees die after they sting their victims.
Unlike honeybees, wasps do not have barbs in their stingers and they can sting over and over again, without dying.

The barbed stinger is connected to the bee's guts.

Honeybees are very helpful to humans and to the world. In addition to making honey, they help pollinate many plants. Pollination involves taking pollen from flower to flower so that plants can reproduce. Without bees and other insects, there would be no plants . . . and then no animals . . . and then no humans!

Honey is a super tasty subject. It is basically made by bees swallowing nectar and barfing it back up. *Delicious!*

Honey has been used for many purposes throughout history. As medicine, people once put it on wounds to prevent infections. Honey has so much sugar, it actually kills most bacteria. The sugar sucks out the water in the bacteria and dehydrates them, but our big bodies can handle this sugar load without problems. There is one particular bacterium that can survive in honey, and it is responsible for a disease called botulism. Normally, botulism spores in honey are only dangerous to babies, so they should not eat honey. Bigger people like you and me have strong enough stomach juices to fend off the spores and keep us safe. If you are old enough to read this book, you can probably gargle down loads of honey without getting botulism, but watch out for tooth cavities! Dangerous botulism bacteria can sometimes grow in canned foods, but canned foods you buy in the store have been cooked to kill the bacteria, making them generally safe.

Killer Bees

Killer bees are mean! They do not have any more venom than North American bees, but they attack in giant swarms and defend their hives much more fiercely. A bunch of killer bees stinging all at once puts a lot more venom into a person than a single bee sting, and that is what makes them so dangerous.

The psycho-ax bee flies solo.
Killer bees attack as a team.

Why are killer bees so mean? Killer bees are hybrids, or a mix of two species. In this case, people mixed European honeybees with African bees, which gives the killer bees another name: Africanized bees.

Killer bees are hybrids.

African bees were brought to South America with the hope of making better honeybees for the tropical climate. However, the bees were not any better at making honey and just ended up keeping their aggressive characteristics. You can't blame them—African bees had to be fierce because they lived in a place where everyone was trying to steal their honey. They had to protect their sweet treasure!

Killer bees have made their way north from South America all the way to the southern United States. But they do not do too well in the cold, so that's about as far north as they have gotten.

Most honeybees you see in North America are nicer because many of them originally come from Europe, where they were bred to be nice. That is, nicer bees were mated with each other, allowing this characteristic to survive. Europeans did this because they worked with the bees to produce honey, and the beekeepers didn't like being stung.

I'm sorry, Mr. Hardcore Penitentiary Bee. Only the nice bees are allowed to make babies.

AVOIDING A SWARM OF KILLER BEES

If you are being chased by a swarm of killer bees, try to get indoors as soon as possible to seal yourself off. When outside, you can run through tall grasses or trees to give yourself more cover from the bees. Never jump in a pool of water because they will wait for you to come out and then sting you. Hopefully you will never have to use this advice.

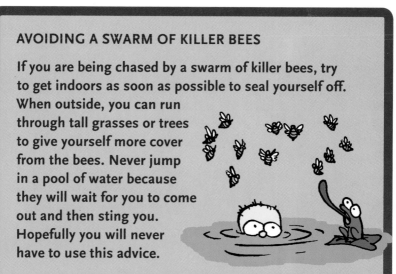

Wasps

The family *Vespidae* includes yellow jackets, hornets, and wasps. Watch out for them! They can be much crankier than their bee counterparts, plus they can sting multiple times. And when they sting, they release a pheromone, which is a chemical that sends a message. This particular pheromone tells the other wasps on the same team to also come sting!

Yellow jackets are probably responsible for most of the "bee stings" that people get. They also cause the most allergic reactions to stings in the United States (see Allergic Reactions, page 36).

Yellow jackets actually like eating meats and sweets, so you often see them buzzing around garbage cans. They can also be annoying when you are trying to have a picnic, especially in the late summer.

I just love a good picnic!

Yellow jackets are not all bad. No, they are not great pollinators like the bees, but they eat many pesty and harmful insects.

Ants

Ants are related to bees and wasps. They belong to the same order—*Hymenoptera*. All ants can bite, but the ant that most often causes painful "bites" in North America is the fire ant.

Like killer bees, fire ants are foreigners brought in by humans and are more aggressive than other ants. They attack in a big mass if their nests are disturbed. Also, they don't just bite, they sting with their butts repeatedly—just like wasps! Fire ants are a pest not only because they bite people, but because they also dig up plant roots for their nests and eat helpful bugs that pollinate plants. Fire ants are common in the Southern states.

This fire ant is not only annoying, he is also a liar.

Velvet Ants

These "ants" are actually a type of wasp. Their stings are so painful that they have earned the nickname "cow kill-ers." Their stings are not actually powerful enough to kill a cow, or a human, but they are among the most painful of all the wasp stings in the United States. Seeing a flying velvet ant may be scary, but don't worry. Flying velvet ants do not sting—only the males can fly and only the females sting. Velvet ants are found mostly in the South and the West.

Note the hairy warning colors on the velvet ant.

I'm killing the cows with my good looks.

Anaphylaxis:
Big-Time Allergic Reactions

Some people are allergic to bee stings so badly that their whole body has a reaction, called anaphylaxis. If not treated, this can sometimes be a life-threatening condition.

What is to blame for this nasty allergic reaction? Your own immune system! Yes, the very system that protects you from most of the nasty microscopic bacteria, viruses, and fungi in the world.

Your immune system is a team of many different cells that patrol your body for anything that does not belong— your personal bodyguards.

Your immune system is a well-coordinated team of cells fighting germy crime.

The first time your body sees a foreign invader, it might not know what to do. After some practice, your body gets really good at knowing how to react and can quickly get rid of that particular bad guy. For example, you only get chicken pox once because after the first time, your body "remembers" how to defend against it. However, you still get colds all the time because there are many different types of cold viruses. Since cold viruses are always changing, they always look like something new to the body.

The immune system has to see things more than once to mount a really good attack.

An allergic reaction occurs when the body is confused and attacks something that may not be so dangerous. Just like with other foreign invaders, the body has to "see" and "remember" the invader before it can launch its giant attack. Unfortunately, this attack can be so giant that it makes you sick!

ANAPHYLAXIS IS A DANGEROUS, WHOLE-BODY REACTION.

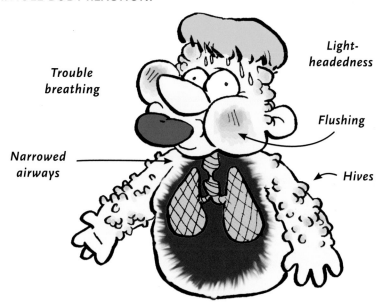

Trouble breathing

Light-headedness

Flushing

Narrowed airways

Hives

During a big-time allergic reaction—anaphylaxis—the team of immune cells releases chemicals that can cause itchy bumps all over the body (hives), difficulty breathing, low blood pressure, and possibly death. In the case of bee stings, the body is confused into thinking the venom is much worse than it really is. Usually it takes at least two stings to get a giant allergic reaction; the first time, the body is not organized enough to launch the full-scale attack. Sometimes it only takes two stings. Sometimes it takes a hundred before the immune system decides to mount its attack.

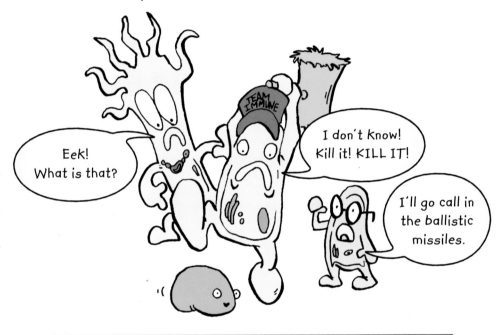

In allergic reactions, the immune system overreacts to things that might not be so harmful.

The most common causes for these giant allergic reactions are foods, medicines, and insect stings. Poison ivy, which was mentioned earlier, causes a different type of allergic reaction that does not lead to anaphylaxis.

So why does the immune system get confused and go crazy? The immune system has to recognize and protect against a million-gazillion different things. That's not easy.

Most of the time, the immune system does a good job of figuring out which are the bad guys, and it launches an appropriate attack.

We should thank our immune systems for keeping us happy and healthy. It is a good idea to know what to do when a giant allergic reaction happens, though, so we can get the right help. People who have had bad allergic reactions in the past should carry an epinephrine pen, which is a shot that can save their life if such a reaction happens. They should also be taken to the hospital as soon as possible.

How to Not Get Stung

Simple answer: don't get too close to stinging insects.

1. Be careful in places with lots of bees and wasps. Picnic sites often have wasps. Bees like flower patches.

2. Don't flail your hands or suddenly dash away if you see a bee or wasp. These quick motions can alarm the insect and provoke an attack. *Stay calm!*

3. Make sure your garbage is nice and neat and that the lid is securely fastened on the can. Of course, don't leave rotting food lying around.

4. Wear light colors. Bees are more attracted to dark colors. Beekeepers usually wear light-colored suits.

5. Be careful of what you smell like when you are in areas where wasps like to hang out. Don't wear flowery perfumes. Bees and wasps are attracted to those smells. Anything with a strong smell can get you in trouble, such as shampoo, aftershave, and sunblock.

6. If a bee "head butts" you (flies straight into you without stinging), you may want to walk back in the direction you came from. Head butting is often a warning that you are getting too close to the hive.

Treating a Sting

Stings can cause pain, swelling, and redness, which usually go away in a few hours to a few days.

If stung by a bee, remove the stinger. The best way is to knock the stinger off using a quick, sideways motion, away from the direction that the stinger is pointing. This can be done by flicking, or swiping the area with a stiff card. **DO NOT** use tweezers or try to pull it out because squeezing the stinger might actually squeeze *more* venom into the wound.

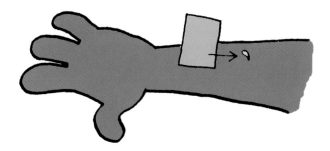

The pain from a sting may be relieved with some meat tenderizer and a warm, moist wrapping. Meat tenderizer may break down some of the venom. Antihistamines that you can buy at the store may also help ease the discomfort. Good ol' ice can help too.

People who know that they are highly sensitive to stings should see a doctor upon getting stung. (See Anaphylaxis, page 36.) Sting-sensitive people should also have an epinephrine pen, which is basically a shot of adrenaline. This shot could save their lives!

Other Venomous Buggeroos

Centipedes

A centipede has a pair of venomous claws on its head that can deliver a painful, though usually not dangerous, bite. Many people believe that the two leglike things sticking out of the butt-end of centipedes actually deliver the venom, but that is incorrect. The head is the venomous end.

The word "centipede" literally means one hundred legs. Most centipedes actually have fewer than one hundred legs, but they all have one pair of legs per body segment. Unlike centipedes, millipedes have two pairs of legs per body segment. Millipedes do not have any venom.

Which one is the centipede?

Moths and Butterflies

What? Butterflies dangerous? Say it ain't so! It ain't so.

Butterflies and moths belong to the order *Lepidoptera*, which literally means "scale winged." The beautiful colors on butterflies and moths come from light reflecting off these scales. The scales might also serve other purposes, such as tasting bad to predators, helping with flight, and regulating body temperature. They may even help with escape from spider webs! Some people are allergic to these powdery scales, and will itch if they touch them.

Moths have scales, not dandruff.

Gross

Unlike the adults, some baby moths and butterflies, also known as caterpillars, might have poisonous spines that can cause itching or pain. If the spines get stuck to your hand, you can take a piece of tape and "stick" them out. Calamine lotion and antihistamines may help with the itching. Most caterpillars do *not* have poisonous spines and are safe to touch.

Lo moth caterpillar

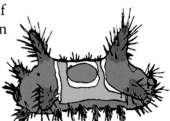

Saddleback caterpillar

Blister Beetles

When threatened, these beetles will play dead and squeeze some red goo from their legs. The goo is called cantharidin and is poisonous when eaten. As the name of the beetle implies, this goo can also cause blisters in humans. It has actually been used medicinally to help remove warts.

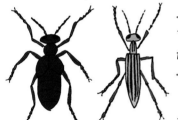

There are over three hundred types of blister beetles. Here are two.

Blister beetle goo has also been used in the past as an aphrodisiac. An aphrodisiac is kind of like a love potion, a substance that makes people want to smooch. People might have thought the goo had romantic properties because the male blister beetles give the females a present of goo after mating. The females actually smear the poisonous goo around their eggs for protection.

Thanks, I've wanted to get rid of that thing for so long!

Fleas

Fleas can jump . . . and jump high! A quarter-inch flea can jump up to a foot, which is like a person jumping 125 feet!

Flea bites are likely to be super itchy. Fleas usually bite around the ankle area, a comfortable height for them to jump.

You can't really feel a flea biting you, but they do get some of their saliva into the bite, which causes a very itchy reaction. Fully grown adult fleas can sometimes live up to a year without eating. That can make these annoying guests hard to get out of your house.

Flea saliva is what makes the bite itchy.

People who have flea problems typically also have pets. Keep your pets away from wild and stray animals. Fleas that bite your pets might also bite you!

Fleas do not really spread many diseases in the United States. In other areas around the world, they are known to spread typhus and are also responsible for the bubonic plague.

Bubonic Plague

The bubonic plague is a famous bacterial disease that killed many people in Europe and Asia throughout history. It is a disease that mainly affects rodents and people, and it can be spread by fleas. Epidemics (new instances of lots of people dying) can start when wild rodents start mingling with city rodents, such as rats, and spread their infected fleas. When the city rodents die, the hungry fleas may find people to infect. Bubonic plague symptoms include fever, swollen lymph nodes, black discolorations on the skin, and lung infections.

There is not a giant plague right now, probably because we have better hygiene and cleaner cities. However, the disease does still exist around the world. In North America, cases of plague occur mainly in the southwestern United States. Squirrels and prairie dogs carry the disease and campers who come in contact with them can get it, although this now occurs rarely. It is serious if a human catches the disease, but it can be successfully treated with antibiotics.

This is how you might get bubonic plague in America.

A creepy and interesting interpretation of the popular rhyme "Ring Around the Rosies" is its association with the bubonic plague. Here are a few examples of the connection.

"Ring around the rosies" may refer to the red, circular rash that pops up as a symptom of the disease.

"Pocket full of posies" may refer to the flowers people kept in their pockets to ward off the stench from dying people.

"Ashes, ashes" may refer to the sneezing sound, "Ah-tishoo," or the ashes from cremated bodies.

"We all fall down" may refer to dying from the disease.

Scary! While interesting to think about, many scholars think the rhyme really has nothing to do with the disease.

Lice

Lice are tiny, flat insects that like to suck blood. Humans can have several types of lice, including ones that like to live in your hair, ones that live on your body, and even ones that live in the underpants area.

Lice are not so much a wilderness danger, but they are a big deal in schools, where wild children lurk. The most common lice for children are head lice. In fact, after virus infections like colds, lice is the second most common contagious problem in elementary school kids.

Communicable disease: a disease that can be "shared."

Unlike fleas, lice are very picky and like to stick to one type of animal. In other words, you most likely cannot give your human lice to your pet, and your pet cannot give its lice to you!

Lice can be shared when people share combs, clothes, headphones, or beds. They cannot jump!

How do you know if you have lice? The only sure way to know is if you see the actual insects in your hair. However, they are very small and can move pretty quickly, so they are often difficult to find. Another way is to find the eggs, which are called nits. They are white and stick to the hair.

Having lice does not mean someone is dirty. It just means they met someone else with lice.

Louse laying an egg on a hair shaft.

When do lice need to be treated? When they are super itchy! There are special shampoos and combs that your doctor might recommend if you have lice. Additionally, things that a person has touched (such as clothes, stuffed animals, and furniture) can be washed or just covered up. Lice cannot survive more than two days when they fall off a human—they dry up! Lice do not necessarily have to be treated if a person does not have symptoms.

SOME THINGS THAT CAN BE MISTAKEN FOR NITS.

Dandruff   **Hair spray residue**   **The root sheath of your hair**

But unlike these other white flecks, nits are cemented to the hair and are very difficult to remove.

School

Kids should *not* miss too much school just because they have lice. They should at least be allowed back after their first treatment. Lots of kids who have lice do not even know it. Head lice are unlikely to cause disease or anything bad. School is too important to miss just because of lice.

Mosquitoes

Mosquitoes are important to talk about because of their ability to spread disease. Did you know that only female mosquitoes bite? Mosquitoes live on nectar, like bees. However, when the females make eggs, they need protein, which nectar has very little of. That's when they supplement their diet with their walking protein shakes, better known as humans and other animals.

What we look like to female mosquitoes: walking protein shakes.

In the rest of the world, mosquitoes can carry malaria, a bad disease. However, in the United States, this is not much of a problem. In the United States, mosquitoes do spread some viruses, such as the West Nile virus and other similar diseases. Most of the time these diseases do not cause symptoms, or just cause flulike symptoms, but occasionally they can lead to more worrisome conditions.

Waves of concern pop up here and there when it seems as if there is a mini-epidemic. If you pay attention to the news, you may have a better idea of when and where to be more cautious. Fewer people die of these diseases than the common flu every year. Most of the time, mosquito bites do not result in much harm, only a lot of itching!

Some people are afraid that since mosquitoes suck blood, they may be able to carry HIV (the virus that causes AIDS). This has *not* been shown to be true.

Mmmmm! What's that you're spreading? Nectar jam?

Around the world, mosquitoes have spread many types of diseases.

Nah, I'm just spreading a little bit of disease.

Why Does a Mosquito Bite Itch?

A mosquito bite is a minor allergic reaction. You cannot feel a mosquito bite because it sticks an extremely thin straw into your skin. Then it releases some proteins through its saliva that prevent your blood from clotting, keeping the blood soupy for slurping.

Unfortunately, most humans are also slightly allergic to these proteins. Most often, the reaction is an itchy bump called a hive or a wheal. Some people who are bitten enough can develop an immunity, and they are lucky enough to have less reactions over time.

This body is reacting to a mosquito bite.

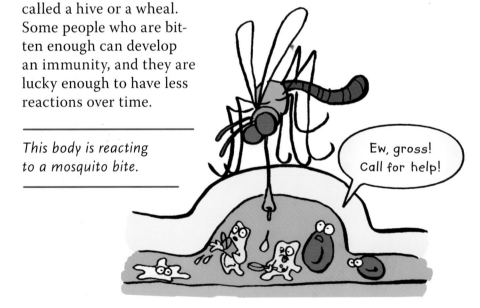

Ew, gross! Call for help!

Treating Mosquito Bites

The best treatment for a mosquito bite is to wash it with soap and water and *not scratch it*! If you have the willpower to resist the urge, it will go away much faster. You can also use calamine lotion or other anti-itch creams, and ice will decrease the itching and swelling.

Poor form.

Avoiding Mosquitoes

Some of the same tips for avoiding bees also apply to mosquitoes, including not wearing bright colors and not wearing anything too fragrant. Here are some additional tips:

1. Have screen doors at your house to keep the bugs out.

2. Get rid of standing water. Mosquito babies live in water that is lying still. Turn empty cans upside down so that they do not catch water. Or better yet, recycle those cans!

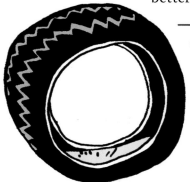

Old tires are famous for holding standing water.

3. When outside in mosquito country, use bug repellent. Bug repellent with DEET is the best. It is best to spray this on clothes. Try not to get too much on your skin, especially your face or eyes.

4. Avoid outdoor activities during dusk in the summer.

Mosquitoes actually find their "meals" by smell. They can sense carbon dioxide, sweat, and other gross things that seep out of your skin when you exercise.

DEET is a chemical that will make you smell less to mosquitoes, so they can't find you. Some natural remedies also decrease your smell, including garlic, pine, and citronella. Catnip might be the best natural remedy because mosquitoes really don't like the smell! But DEET may still be the best choice because it is the most effective, works the longest, and will not start a feline frenzy!

_____

Catnip: repels mosquitoes, attracts cats.

_____

Spiders

3

Spiders

There are over three thousand different types of spiders in North America, and *all* of them are venomous. Does that mean you should be worried? No! Spiders need venom to help them catch their food. But most spiders are too small or do not have enough venom to mess you up—you probably would not even feel their bites!

Spiders are arachnids. Arachnids are different from insects in many ways. One is that spiders have eight legs and two body segments while insects have six legs and three body segments. All spiders also have a pair of fangs, known as chelicerae.

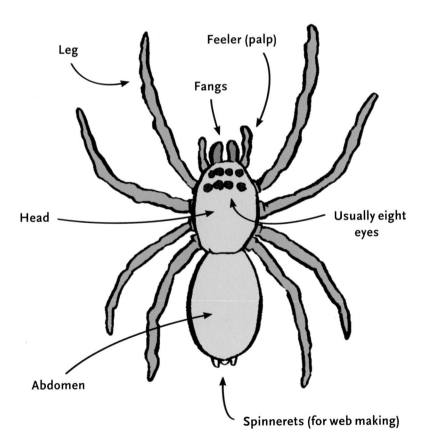

Leg

Feeler (palp)

Fangs

Head

Usually eight eyes

Abdomen

Spinnerets (for web making)

If a spider bites you, you might see a little red bump on your skin, with or without fang marks. The bump may be sore, but should go away in a few days. Occasionally a bite can become infected, but this is less likely to happen if you keep it clean.

Lots of people blame weird bumps on spider bites, even though they never see the spider. Most of the time those mysterious bumps are actually due to other conditions, or are bites from other creepy crawlies such as mosquitoes or bedbugs. North American spiders are not very aggressive and would only bite if they felt really scared or trapped, such as if you accidentally sat on one. Spiders do not actively want to bite you, unlike mosquitoes, which like to suck your blood.

There are only a few spiders in North America that may have dangerous or extra painful bites. These are the black widows, the brown recluses, and the tarantulas. (Bad bites can come from a few other American spiders, but these bites occur so rarely that they will not be discussed in this book.)

Owl! I knew watching *Zombie Chainsaw Mayhem* with a spider was a bad idea!

Spiders only bite when they are really scared.

Black Widows

Can you guess how the black widow spider got its name? It was thought that the female often ate the male after mating, but in nature this rarely ever happens. Usually the male has a good chance of escaping, and the female does not attack unless she is particularly hungry. In a lab, it may be more likely for a male to be eaten because the two spiders are stuck in a small cage together. Outside of the United States, there are other species of widow spiders where females eat their mates more often.

Female black widows are easily recognized by their black bodies and the red hourglass pattern on their abdomens. Males are much smaller than females.

Only female black widows have venom that can hurt humans. Of all North American spiders, their venom is the most worrisome. However, they are shy and rarely bite, unless they are seriously disturbed or if they are protecting their eggs.

If you are bitten by a black widow, you will most likely get a little red bump that might be kind of sore. Not too bad. The worry is that some people may have severe reactions. This starts with muscle spasms, often around the area of the bite, and in the belly. The belly may become painful and stiff as a board. This can progress to a feeling of everything "speeding up," which includes sweating, breathing fast, racing of the heart, throwing up, and feeling confused and acting all crazy. (People might say this happens to them when they fall in love, but these are all bad things in the context of spider bites.)

Lover boy here shows us some features of black widow bites:

Dizzy

Sweating

Racing heartbeat

No smile

Stiff, painful belly

Spasms

Black widows are found in every U.S. state except Alaska. They like to live in sheltered areas—under logs, in fields, and under stones in gardens. The people-places that they like best are garage corners and sheds. Most people are bitten on the hands and feet, but when outhouses were more common, people were often bitten on the butt by spiders hiding under toilet seats.

Augh! My butt!

Maybe I'll hold it a little longer...

Brown Recluse Spiders

Brown recluses like to hang out in houses, hiding in cracks or behind furniture. People rarely see them, because they hide during the day and come out at night. Brown recluses rarely bite people, and even when they do, medical treatment is usually not required. Bites most often happen when a spider is hiding under clothes on the ground or when a person accidentally rolls on top of a spider. Brown recluse spiders are most common in the southern central states.

One reason to clean your room is so spiders don't hide in your clothes.

Bad spider bites may result in a condition called *necrosis*. This is kind of like having your skin melt away into mush,

IDENTIFYING A BROWN RECLUSE

A brown recluse spider is sometimes called a "fiddleback" or "violin" spider because of the violin shape on its front body segment. The drawing here shows that it also can be identified by the lighter color of its abdomen. A brown recluse only has six eyes, arranged in pairs of two. Most spiders have eight eyes.

Brown recluse

and that hurts! It usually does get better, though it may be slow to heal, taking as long as several weeks. However, the bite is not deadly.

Daddy Longlegs

There's an urban legend that daddy longlegs venom is strong enough to kill people, but its fangs are too small to actually do any harm. But this legend is not true.

While daddy longlegs are arachnids, they are *not* spiders and have *zero* venom. They eat decaying plants and are totally harmless. Daddy longlegs only have one body segment, as opposed to spiders, which have two. They also have only two eyes, whereas most spiders have eight.

Yargh!
This here's my shanty:
The real daddy I be.
I have but one segment,
not two, not three.
Back to the cellar with ye,
You imposter, spiderly.

Note: Real daddy longlegs are not rhyming pirates.

One type of spider, the cellar spider, is often incorrectly called a daddy longlegs. It is a spider, as it has two body segments, eight eyes, and venom. It also has very small fangs, but has not been shown to do people any harm.

Cellar spider

Tarantulas

Tarantulas are large, hairy spiders found all over the world where it is warm. In the United States, tarantulas mostly live in the Southwest.

Despite their reputation, tarantulas rarely bite. Like most animals, they may bite if you mess around with them too much. Their bites might be comparable to being stung by a bee, although some bites are so mild that you do not even feel them.

While it is possible to have an allergic reaction to a bite (see Anaphylaxis, page 36), it is far more common to have an allergic or irritating reaction to the hair on their bodies. In sensitive people, the spider hair can cause red, itchy bumps that can last for weeks. (The hair can be pulled off with some tape.) Some tarantulas can kick hairs from their butt onto whoever is annoying them . . . so don't annoy a tarantula!

My accuracy is impeccable!

Looks like your butt could use more ammo, pardner.

TASTE A TARANTULA

I don't think mine's done cooking yet.

The largest spider in the world is a type of tarantula that can grow to the size of a dinner plate! These spiders are large enough to roast and eat, and reportedly they taste like crab or shrimp.

THE TARANTELLA

There is a medieval legend from Italy that claims that people could go crazy and hallucinate if they were bitten by a tarantula. However, in Italy, the "tarantula" is actually the wolf spider, another large, hairy spider. Bite victims were told to do a frantic dance called the "tarantella" to dance away the venom. The tarantella may either be named after the spider or the town of Taranto, Italy, which supposedly had a spider "epidemic."

To add to the confusion, other more venomous spiders probably caused the strange symptoms. Wolf spiders were large and more commonly seen, so they got the blame! The tarantula as we know it probably got its name from explorers to the New World who found the big, hairy spider and named it according to what they knew back home.

Robots doing the tarantella.

Scorpions

Scorpions, like spiders, are arachnids. They have two body segments, eight legs, and mouth parts with the same fancy name: chelicerae. In addition, scorpions have a stinger and claws. The claws are important for catching food and for doing a scorpion mating dance.

Let's get the dance on!

Depending on its size, a scorpion may eat insects or even small lizards. Its stinger injects venom to help the scorpion slow down its prey. The venom also starts digesting the prey so that the scorpion can slurp up the food. Some scorpions only have to eat once a year.

In the United States, scorpions live in the South, mostly the Southwest. Only a few types of these U.S. scorpions can actually cause harm. Their stings may cause burning, pain, and swelling. If a sting is really bad, a person may vomit, drool, and have difficulty breathing, and it can even mess up organs such as the heart and pancreas. In the United States, no one has died of a scorpion sting since 1968, so even if you get stung, you will most likely be OK if you go see a doctor. Antivenin is available for scorpion stings (see page 85 for a description of antivenin). This is reserved for severe reactions to scorpion stings. You can take care of a sting just like you would a spider bite.

Scorpions do not like the light. They are nocturnal animals.

I am definitely not a morning— make that not a day—person.

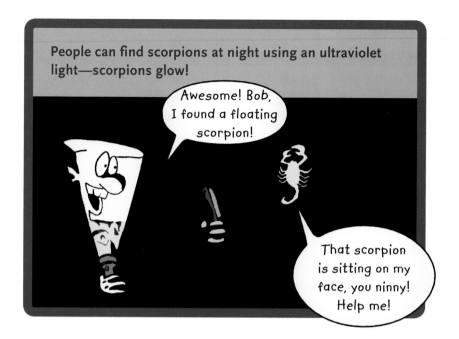

People can find scorpions at night using an ultraviolet light—scorpions glow!

Awesome! Bob, I found a floating scorpion!

That scorpion is sitting on my face, you ninny! Help me!

Whip Scorpions

Whip scorpions might look even scarier than scorpions, if you can imagine that! Like scorpions, they also have claws that can pinch. Despite their looks, they cannot sting and do not have venom like the scorpions do. Instead, they have an odd defense mechanism: they spray ascetic acid, better known as vinegar.

Because of this, some whip scorpions are also known as vinegarones. Although not quite as dangerous as scorpion venom, the ascetic acid they spray is fifteen times stronger than household vinegar, which can be irritating, especially if it gets in your eyes. These nocturnal animals like to hide under rocks and are rarely seen. In the United States, they are found in the Southwest and in Florida.

It's a bit strong!

VINEGAR

Ticks

Like spiders, ticks are arachnids (see page 54). These little creatures are often mistaken for lice or fleas, but they are all different buggeroos! Ticks are important to know about because of their ability to spread diseases. There are many different types of ticks, and not all ticks can transmit diseases to humans.

Ticks are vectors, which means they pass diseases from one animal to another. They can only pass on a disease if they bite another animal that has the disease first. Ticks are known to spread about a dozen different diseases within the United States, including Rocky Mountain spotted fever, tularemia, and, most famously, Lyme disease. Lyme disease is caused by a spiral-shaped bacterium.

Spirochete (swirly bacterium)

To pass on Lyme disease, a tick must bite an infected mouse before biting a human. If you see a tick crawling on you, or even if you are bitten, do not panic! Most ticks are not infected with Lyme disease, and infected ticks may not even pass along the disease. The tick usually needs to be attached to you for at least a whole day before it can give you the disease, so the key is to remove the tick as soon as possible!

Tick Life Cycle

Adult female lays eggs—over three thousand at a time.

Larva hatches.

Larva waits in leaf litter, then latches on to a small mammal or bird and feeds.

Adult waits at tips of grasses and bites passing mammals, including humans.

Larva molts into a nymph. Nymph is as big as the period in this sentence.

Nymph molts and becomes an adult. The adult is still tiny.

Nymph waits in leaf litter, then latches on to a small mammal or bird and feeds. Mice are the primary reservoir for Lyme disease.

Symptoms of Lyme Disease

One characteristic early symptom of Lyme disease is a curious circular rash that forms around the site of the bite. It gets bigger and bigger and may look like a bull's-eye. Lyme disease can also cause pain in the joints or affect the brain, causing headaches, weakness, hallucinations, weird tingly feelings, and seizures. Know what symptoms to look for, and see your doctor if you are concerned.

Antibiotics do an excellent job of treating this disease, especially when it is diagnosed early. Lyme disease is not contagious between humans. Only ticks can transmit the disease—no other buggeroos can do so.

Headache

Fever

Weakness

Spreading, bull's-eye rash

Joint pain

Some symptoms of Lyme disease

Preventing Tick Diseases

To prevent getting diseases from ticks, it is most important to avoid being bitten.

Ticks can get on you when you walk through tall grasses, low-lying shrubs, or leaf litter in the woods. You have to brush into a tick for it to get on you. Ticks cannot jump or fly.

So... close... almost... got... 'im...

Here are a few more safety tips to avoid tick bites.

Tie back long hair.

Use bug spray with DEET or permethrin.

If your pets like to romp in the woods, don't forget to check them for ticks.

Stay on marked trails.

When in tick country, wearing long sleeves helps. Also, tuck your pants into your socks.

After you come home, check your body for ticks, or have a friend help. Be sure to include good hiding places, like your armpits, hair, behind your ears, and groin.

If a tick has bitten you, you can have someone help you pull it off using sharp-pointed tweezers, or even string. Grab the tick as close to its mouth as possible and pull straight out from the skin. Do not squeeze the tick's body or head, because it could squish more guts, saliva, or disease into your body. Then wash the bitten area well and pay attention to any weird symptoms or rashes that develop after the bite. Some people say to use stuff like Vaseline, nail polish, or matches, but these should be avoided because they could make the tick sick and barf disease into you before it is removed.

Pulling out a tick.

Arachnophobia

Some people are *very* afraid of spiders, beyond what is considered typical. This is known as *arachnophobia*. People can have all sorts of phobias. People with phobias might understand the silliness of their fears, but they can't help being totally scared and feeling "doomed."

So how do you know if you actually have a phobia? You might feel shaky, sweaty, anxious, or dizzy, feel a need to run away, or start crying.

There are three general categories of phobias:

1. Social phobias, such as fear of public speaking (glossophobia).

2. Fear of open places or leaving the safety of home (agoraphobia).

3. Specific phobias, which can be fears of anything. More common phobias include fear of spiders (arachnophobia), fear of heights (acrophobia), and the fear of closed-in places (claustrophobia). Many interesting phobias exist, such as the fear of being alone (monophobia), the fear of being buried alive (taphephobia), and the fear of poop (coprophobia).

People have phobias toward spiders more than to any other animal. Why do phobias occur? No one really knows. People who have phobias may be more likely to have an underlying issue with anxiety. Some people may be born more easily scared by spiders, or it could be a result of our culture: we view spiders as "creepy" and "bad," which may lead to us being afraid of them. For example, not too many native Amazonians are afraid of spiders—they *eat* spiders! Amazonians are no more afraid of spiders than we are of Brussels sprouts.

Can phobias be treated? Yes! The best treatment includes behavioral therapy. People are taught to relax, and then they are slowly exposed to more and more of what frightens them until they are not so scared anymore. Techniques might include talking about fears, slowly experiencing one's phobias, and even virtual reality.

Spider Bite Care

With all bites, it is important to clean the site of the wound with soap (see Wound Infections on page 90). You can use ice to control the pain and swelling. You may also want to see a doctor if you know a dangerous spider has bitten you, if severe reactions occur, or if the bite is not healing. Dancing the tarantella is not necessary.

Again, the spider bite of most concern may be that of the black widow, although black widow bites are uncommon. Brown recluse spiders can live safely among people, although you would need to treat a necrotic bite. And while tarantula bites may be painful, they are generally less worrisome than the bites of the above two spiders.

Exploring Spiders

It is fun to explore and learn about spiders. Don't be scared! Spiders are very helpful, eating a lot of other insects that might cause damage or be annoying to humans. You can best find spiders at night, behind cupboards or under the cellar stairs.

Use a flashlight—lots of times, spiders are easy to find because their eyes light up like bicycle reflectors! To get started, practice looking for spiders at the bottom of the page. How many can you find? I can find eighty-four . . . but you're doing pretty good if you find twenty.

Amphibians and Reptiles

4

Amphibians and Reptiles

Amphibians and reptiles are four-legged, cold-blooded animals with backbones. Interestingly, both groups have some animals that appear to not have legs, such as snakes and legless lizards (reptiles), and caecilians (amphibians).

REPTILES

Lizards Turtles Alligators Snakes

AMPHIBIANS

Frogs and toads Salamanders and newts

Skin

It is generally safe to touch the skins of North American amphibians and reptiles, although you might have to watch out for bites, especially from reptiles. Not only do many reptiles have sharp teeth, some also have venom!

Many amphibians produce mucus from their skin, making them slimy. Reptiles, on the other hand, always have dry, scaly skin. Many amphibians also have poison glands in their skin.

Snakes are reptiles. They are not slimy . . . unless you do something gross like blow your nose on them.

The poison glands in North American amphibians are not strong enough to hurt you if you pick them up. Amphibian poison can make the animals taste bad or make predators sick, forcing them to think twice about eating amphibians.

I'll get you, you whippersnapper!

You don't have to worry about bites from most commonly seen North American amphibians. Frogs have small, weak teeth only on the top their mouths. Land salamanders have teeth on the top and bottom of their mouths, but they're small and not dangerous.

Toads secrete poison from their parotid glands, the big bumps behind their eyes. Despite the poison, it is safe to pick up a toad, though you should wash your hands afterward and avoid touching your mouth or eyes. Also, be prepared for a wet surprise: wild toads often pee when you pick them up. The pee is mostly water and will not hurt you.

Toads also have "warts," which are just bumps on their skin. People *cannot* get warts from touching toads. People warts are caused by viruses.

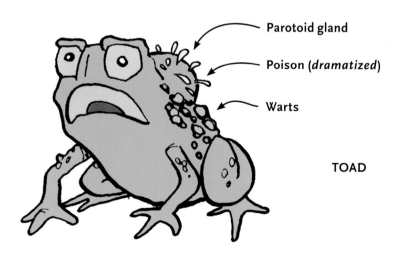

Parotoid gland

Poison (*dramatized*)

Warts

TOAD

You are lucky that the largest organ of your body, your skin, protects you from countless dangers. You can safely touch mild poisons, such as amphibian skin, without getting sick. However, you should try not to get any in your mouth, on your face, or in your eyes. It is *always* a good idea to wash your hands after touching any animal.

Skin: awesome protection.

Salmonella

As good as skin is, you should still wash up with soap after touching any animal—even beloved pets! One well-known germ that many pet reptiles carry is salmonella, which is a bacterium that can cause food poisoning. Sure, the bacteria is thwarted by your skin, but if you swallow it, you can get fevers, vomiting, and bloody diarrhea.

Salmonella is found in the intestines and poop of reptiles. Pet reptiles might have more salmonella on their bodies than those found in the wild because they are stuck in a small cage. Their poop is also stuck in that small cage, so they are likely to have much more of that bacteria on their bodies than wild animals.

Earlier in the day . . .

I love you pookie snookums!

Ugh, I should've washed my hands...

You might want to wash your whole body, junior.

Poison Dart Frogs

I need more juice, boy! This sloth is a relentless beast!

Poison dart frogs are amphibians that live in South America. Native tribesmen dip their darts and arrows in poison from the frogs' skin to help them hunt. The most poisonous frog is the golden poison dart frog, *Phyllobates terribilis.* Just touching this frog with your skin or mouth may cause numbness or burning. If the poison gets into an open wound, it could kill a human. In fact, one frog has enough poison to kill one hundred people! Some North American amphibians may also be deadly if eaten, but they are all generally safe to touch.

Phyllobates terribilis *may be the most poisonous amphibian. The red eft is a poisonous North American newt. You can tell by the warning color. It is nowhere as poisonous as a poison dart frog.*

Exploring Amphibians

Wet places—ponds and marshes—are good places to find amphibians. Some live in the water, and some like to hide under rocks and logs. Nighttime may be the best time to find or listen to amphibians. How many different frog calls can you hear?

If you pick up an amphibian, please be kind and do not hold it for too long. Do not let it dry out! Some amphibians actually do a lot of their breathing through their skin, and they need to stay moist to live.

Dried up amphibians are not happy . . . and oftentimes not alive.

Snakessss SSSsssSSSssss

All snakes are predators, and yes, they do bite. Many snakes use constriction to catch their prey, even little ones. In North America, there is no snake big enough (or gutsy enough) to try squishing you to death, so all you have to watch out for are bites. If bitten, you can consult "Wound Infections" on page 90 or "Bites" on page 99. But the focus here is on the most worrisome of bites: venomous bites.

You can learn how to identify venomous and nonvenomous snakes. There are two families of venomous snakes in North America: pit vipers (*Crotalidae*) and coral snakes (*Elapidae*). Most venomous species in North America belong

SOME STRATEGIES THAT SNAKES USE TO CATCH PREY.

Venom

I just want **one** anchovy!

Constriction

Do you need insurance?

Incognito (wait and strike)

Omigosh!

Racing/Chasing

to the pit viper family. They can be easily identified because most have rattles. The other group, coral snakes, is very easy to identify by their colorful bands (see page 82).

Here are a few features you can use to tell venomous from nonvenomous snakes in North America.

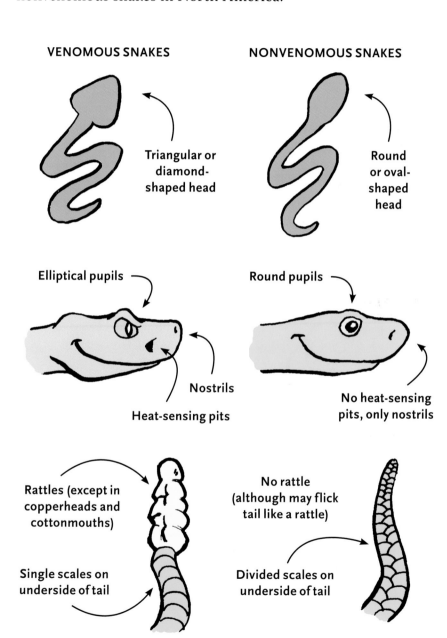

VENOMOUS SNAKES

Triangular or diamond-shaped head

Elliptical pupils

Nostrils

Heat-sensing pits

Rattles (except in copperheads and cottonmouths)

Single scales on underside of tail

NONVENOMOUS SNAKES

Round or oval-shaped head

Round pupils

No heat-sensing pits, only nostrils

No rattle (although may flick tail like a rattle)

Divided scales on underside of tail

Biting Snakes

Why do snakes bite? They're scared! Snakes in North America would much rather hide or slither away than bite a human. They would prefer to save their venom for their prey, rather than waste it on self-defense. It takes a snake a few weeks to fill up its venom tank again. Also, snakes are pretty fragile and their bones can easily be broken, so they really don't want to be picking any fights with people. Often, snakes bite as a warning to scare off potential harm.

Most of the venomous snakebites in North America do not cause death when properly treated. The venom is designed to kill small animals that the snakes eat, and people are really *big* animals. Luckily, humans are harder to kill that way, but you still need to be careful.

Snakes do not always inject their venom when they bite. When they bite their prey, they can figure out how much venom to inject based on the size of the animal. When biting humans, rattlesnakes sometimes do not even inject their venom.

I'm gonna have to pump up the venom for this delicious entree...

Snake venom glands are found underneath their eyes. The venom is squirted out through the fangs. This snake is half full . . . or half empty.

Pit Vipers

Pit vipers are scary-looking venomous snakes with big fangs and angry eyes. If you can look past their grumpy faces, you'll see that like many other snakes, they actually have beautiful body patterns. All pit vipers in North America are rattlesnakes, except for the cottonmouth and copperhead.

Rattles

Many snakes vibrate their tails as a warning, and rattle-snakes have actual "rattles" that make the warnings louder. All snakes with actual rattles are venomous. Reptiles need to shed their old skin, and the rattles on pit vipers are made from shed skin. Some people think you can tell how old a snake is from its rattle, but this method is not very reliable. Snakes' rattles get longer every time they shed their skins, but it is unpre-dictable how many times in a year a snake might have shed its skin. Also, rattles can break off over time.

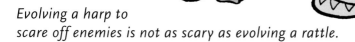

Evolving a harp to scare off enemies is not as scary as evolving a rattle.

Venom

The main problem with pit viper venom is that it eats away at your tissues. A bite might start looking all mushy, like it is being digested. Common reactions include pain, swelling, bleeding underneath the skin, and throwing up. In severe cases, a bite victim will experience internal bleeding, blood clotting problems, difficulty breathing, or kidney failure. However, these complications can be prevented by going to the hospital within a few hours of being bitten. With proper treatment, bites are rarely fatal.

Rattlesnake venom is eating away this blood vessel. The antivenin (AV) team is here to stop them!

Copperheads and Cottonmouths

These are the pit vipers that don't have rattles. In North America, most of the venomous snakebites are from copperheads. They are dangerous, although less venomous than other rattlesnakes, and they are unlikely to cause death.

Copperheads and cottonmouths are very closely related. Sometimes these snakes are called "moccasins." It is true that cottonmouths swim and can bite underwater, making them the feared "water moccasins." However, not all swimming snakes are dangerous, as in the case of the common water snake, which is often mistakenly called a "water moccasin." Sometimes you can tell if a swimming snake is a cottonmouth, because it often holds its head above the water, while other nonvenomous swimming snakes usually swim completely underwater. These snakes are named cottonmouths because when threatened, they open their mouths really big to reveal a shocking white (cotton) mouth.

Copperheads are hard to see in leaf litter . . . so here's one on a pink piano.

Special Snake Senses

Snakes are almost deaf—they have no ears on the outside! However, they have many special senses. For example, when you see a snake stick out its tongue, it is actually *smelling* you! Its tongue flicks in and out, putting the scent in a special organ inside the mouth.

Snakes are also really good at feeling vibrations in the ground, so they know when food or scary things like people are coming. Pit vipers have additional heat-sensing pits in their snouts, allowing them to "see" the heat produced from warm-blooded animals like mice, birds, and people.

Snakes are like ninjas . . . without arms . . . or karate.

Coral Snakes

Most venomous snakes in North America are pit vipers. Coral snakes are an exception to this rule. They are more closely related to cobras, which have very powerful venom. Although coral snakes are dangerous, they are also shy and less likely to bite than rattlesnakes. Most people who get bitten are people who pick these snakes up.

A coral snake bite can cause pain and swelling. More worrisome, coral snake venom is neurotoxic, which means it is poisonous to the nerves and brain. Bite victims may develop numbness and tingling, loss of muscle movement, heart failure, and breathing difficulty. For bite treatments, see "Venomous Snakebite Treatment" on page 84.

Coral snakes have bright, candy-cane patterns that scream, "Don't touch me, I'm dangerous!" Because of this, some other snakes have developed patterns similar to coral snakes for protection, even though they are not dangerous. These include milk snakes and king snakes. One way to tell the two types of snakes apart is this old rhyme:

Red next to black, friend of Jack.
Red next to yellow, kills a fellow.

In this case, coral snakes have a red-next-to-yellow pattern —dangerous! However, this rhyme only works in North America, as the red next to black pattern may be dangerous in the rest of the world. Even if you know this rhyme, it would be smart not to get bitten by any of these snakes, just in case!

Coral snake
(venomous)

Snake pretending to be a
coral snake
(not venomous)

Funkadelic snake
(groovy)

Lizards

Did you know that the two main venomous lizard species in the world live in southwestern North America? They are the Gila monster and the Mexican beaded lizard. Some studies suggest that other lizards may also be venomous, but these guys are undisputed. These lizards can be pretty nasty, because if they bite, they may not let go! They like to keep chewing an area to make sure their venom gets into the wound. Do not mess with these reptiles! These beautiful animals are becoming increasingly rare, so if you find one, leave it be. Both you and the lizards will be safer that way.

People who are bitten by these lizards will have pain and swelling at the site, and sometimes feel weak or faint. The bites are generally less serious than snakebites. As with any bites, make sure to thoroughly clean the wound area. Check that teeth and other debris are removed. Your doctor can tell you if you need a tetanus shot (see page 97). Clean the area daily.

Don't mess with Gila jaws.

Venomous Snakebite Treatment

If you have been bitten by a pit viper, and there is no intense pain within seconds, nor lots of swelling within minutes, the snake probably did not inject any venom. However, this is *not* the case with coral snakes.

Follow these simple rules if you've just been bitten by a possibly venomous snake:

1. Avoid panic. Get away from the snake to avoid getting bitten again. If possible, try to remember what the snake looks like so that an expert can identify it and decide what needs to be done. There is no need to catch or kill the snake.

2. Try to move the bitten arm or leg as little as possible. The best way to do that is to make a splint. The less you move, the less the wound will be damaged, and the less poison will be absorbed by your body. Remove jewelry like rings and bracelets to allow for swelling.

A splint uses something stiff to prevent your joints from moving.

3. Get help!

4. Keep drinking fluids, a little bit at a time. This helps to make sure there is enough fluid in your blood vessels and your kidneys.

5. In the case of a coral snake, you may tie the area above the bite with a piece of cloth or something elastic. You should tie it not too tight and not too loose, but just enough for one finger to slip through. Do *not* make it super tight like a tourniquet! In the case of rattlesnakes and copperheads, compression will not help.

6. See a doctor!

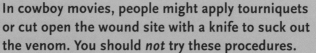

In cowboy movies, people might apply tourniquets or cut open the wound site with a knife to suck out the venom. You should *not* try these procedures.

Also, as opposed to most animal bites, do *not* ice snakebites! These methods can all do more harm than good.

Cowboy doctor

Antivenin

The doctor may consider treating a snakebite with antivenin, which is a protein that binds to the venom like a straitjacket, not letting it do any damage.

Antivenin is often made from horses. Horses are big animals (bigger than people), so they can be injected with some snake venom without it hurting them. The horse's body will respond by making proteins, or antivenin, to help get rid of the venom.

If you need antivenin, you will get a shot of the horse's serum, or the watery part of the blood. One problem is that people can be allergic to horse proteins, and develop serum sickness. This can cause rashes, fever, and joint pain. Often, serum sickness is worse than getting bitten by a venomous snake! That is why a doctor has to be very careful about giving antivenin. Most people do not need antivenin and can get better by themselves. Antivenin is given only for severe bite cases.

I totally hate this job.

Making antivenin

Tips for Avoiding Snakebites

Keep your eyes out on warm days. Snakes are more active when it is above seventy degrees. More snakes live in the South because it is warmer.

Wear long pants and thick, sturdy shoes. A pair of pants might be just enough protection to deflect a snakebite. And always have a buddy hike with you.

Learn what venomous snakes look like. You can find out which ones live in your area from books, nature centers, or park rangers.

Snakes like to hide under rocks and logs. Be careful when picking up things on the ground that might make good hiding spots. Definitely don't stick your hands in cracks where you cannot see. Also, when you walk by a log on a trail, you can jump off the log rather than stepping over it.

Mammals

5

Mammals

Mammals are animals that are warm-blooded, have hair, and give milk. There are no poisonous mammals, and only a few venomous mammals.

Two general types of mammals have venom:

1. Some shrews, and the solenodon (a Caribbean shrewlike creature), have venomous bites.

2. The duck-billed platypus has a venomous spur on the back of each leg.

No horseback rides for platypuses.

In both cases, the venom can cause extreme, long-lasting pain, burning, and swelling, but these will generally go away. Lucky for you, neither the solenodon nor the platypus can be found attacking people in the United States, and there have been no reported American shrew bites since the 1930s.

3. There is a third "venomous" mammal in an odd category of its own: the slow loris. It makes a toxin with its armpit. The loris licks this toxin up to deliver a mildly venomous bite, or spreads the toxin on its babies to ward off predators. Lorises live in Southeast Asia.

Cartoons tell the truth! Twelve out of every one thousand postal workers are bitten by a dog every year. However, of everybody, kids are bitten the most often. So kids, be careful!

You're next, buddy.

Pretty obviously, the most likely way for you to get hurt by a mammal is by being bitten. In the United States, people are bitten more by dogs and cats than any other mammals.

Rounding out the top four mammalian biters after dogs and cats are rodents and . . . humans. Yikes! Better watch out for the dude sitting next to you.

This chapter will focus on what you need to worry about with mammal bites. It will not dwell on obvious stuff, such as, "Don't go petting wild grizzly bears." As a rule of thumb, you should avoid touching any wild mammal unless you are with an expert.

Wound Infections

What is an infection? An infection is when something starts growing where it is not supposed to be growing. This growth can cause damage to the surrounding body area.

A wound infection is an infection of the skin and the surrounding flesh, usually caused by bacteria. Bacteria naturally grow on top of your skin, and that is normal. However, skin can get infected when it is cut open and the bacteria get inside. Bacteria are not supposed to be found under the skin, which is why it is so important to clean any cuts or scrapes you might have.

Classic wound infection

How can you tell if you have a wound infection? The wound may become swollen, hot, really red all

Normal body cell

Bacterium

around, hurt a lot, and have pus oozing out. If you have a fever after being bitten, give your doctor a holler.

Bacteria naturally grow on the parts of your body that are in contact with the outside world. This includes your skin and your whole gastrointestinal (GI) tract, which comes in contact with all of the food you eat. The GI tract includes your mouth, esophagus, stomach, intestines, and butt. The rest of your body is totally "clean," which means that normally, no bacteria grow in it.

The bacteria on your skin and in your GI tract are harmless where they are, and often very helpful! You need them— some bacteria are even necessary for survival, like the ones that help digest your food. However, these bacteria become harmful when they are in the wrong places. They are not supposed to live in your blood, muscles, brain, bones, or other organs. When they start growing in those areas, that is considered an infection, and that's trouble!

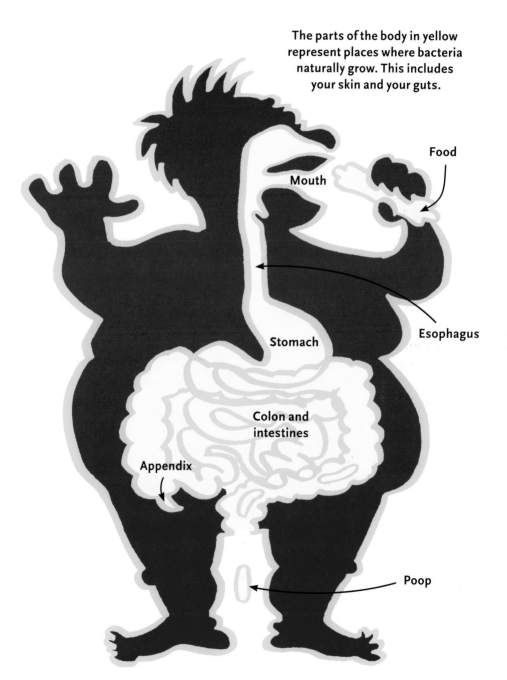

The parts of the body in yellow represent places where bacteria naturally grow. This includes your skin and your guts.

Food

Mouth

Esophagus

Stomach

Colon and intestines

Appendix

Poop

Pet Bites

Here's a question: are you more likely to get an infection from a cat bite or a dog bite? If you looked at the illustration on this page, you probably said CATS!

You are much more likely to get an infection from a cat bite than a dog bite because of the things that like to grow in cat mouths. You can get infections from the bites of any animal, but some animals are more likely to give you infections. These include pigs and large wild carnivores (like lions and bears, oh my!) . . . and guess what might even be worse?

HUMANS!

That's right, we're disgusting, even those of us who brush our teeth. Regardless, you should treat all these bites with equal care, starting with a nice, thorough washing.

Does that mean we can't be kissed or licked by our furry (and not-so-furry) friends? No, don't worry, it's OK. Bites are bad because they break through your skin and let bacteria get into places they are not supposed to be. It's fine to get licked and kissed, but try not to get licked or kissed by anything or anyone that is sick or barfing.

Cat Scratch Fever

When someone has a fever and huge, swollen lymph nodes, doctors may think about cat scratch fever. Guess how you get the disease? (Psst! The name of the disease tells you the answer!) Interestingly, it is more likely to be passed on by bites or scratches from kittens. Usually the disease is not too bad, but sometimes it can last a long time. Cat scratch fever can be treated with antibiotics.

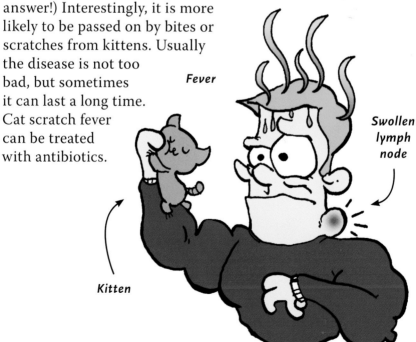

Fever

Swollen lymph node

Kitten

Rabies

Imagine you were just bitten by a mammal—will you get rabies?

Not likely. On average, less than three people die of rabies each year in the United States. Although it is uncommon, rabies is a bad disease that can kill, so that is why doctors are careful about rabies in people who have been bitten.

So what is rabies? It's a virus that is spread through the saliva of an infected mammal, usually a carnivore. Nonmammals, such as reptiles, fish, and insects, do not get rabies. The virus travels up the nerves, up the spinal cord, all the way up to the brain. Once the virus gets to the brain, it reproduces itself very quickly, and then gets into the saliva. Rabies can kill animals (and people) very quickly, anywhere from a few days to a couple of weeks.

The path of rabies

When someone gets rabies, at first it will seem like they have the flu—fever, headache, and feeling yucky. The bite site might feel tingly. In a few days, the person gets more and more anxious, nervous, and confused. The person may start to hallucinate, act strangely, and have trouble sleeping. Large amounts of saliva may be produced and the person cannot swallow, resulting in a "foaming at the mouth" appearance. Unfortunately, once it gets to this point, the disease is usually not curable.

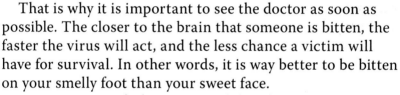

Don't forget to wash very well with soap the site where you have been bitten. Soap is very good at killing the rabies virus! (Don't wash your mouth with detergent, unless you want people to think you have rabies.)

That is why it is important to see the doctor as soon as possible. The closer to the brain that someone is bitten, the faster the virus will act, and the less chance a victim will have for survival. In other words, it is way better to be bitten on your smelly foot than your sweet face.

However, even if a biting animal does have rabies, a bitten person may not necessarily get the disease. It depends on how much virus is in the animal's saliva, and how much actually gets into the person's system. If doctors think that a biting animal has rabies, a series of shots that are very good at getting rid of the disease can be given to the victim.

Raccoons, skunks, and bats are the animals most likely to spread rabies in North America. Most of them do not have rabies, so don't go starting an antiraccoon mob!

However, it is important to maintain a safe distance from these wild animals. Animals are pretty awesome and can be safely enjoyed from afar. Few domesticated animals (such as your pet cat or dog) get rabies because they are vaccinated. Humans are not usually vaccinated because they do not meet up with possibly rabid wild animals as often as their pets do. But people who handle animals—zookeepers and veterinarians—have to get the rabies shot.

If you love your pet, make sure he gets all his shots.

Don't worry if you have not been vaccinated for rabies. It is unlikely that any wild mammal will try to touch you or attack you. Most wild animals are afraid of people and will try to stay away or out of sight. Some city mammals, like squirrels, might get used to people and may not be as afraid of you getting close. However, if a wild mammal approaches you, be careful! It might be mad about you stepping foot in its territory, or it might have another problem, like rabies. This may not always be the case, but resist the cuteness and keep yourself safe!

Avoid wild animals that are unusually "friendly."

Tetanus

Tetanus is a terrible condition that can cause muscles to go stiff or spasm. This can make it difficult to move and breathe, and can even result in death.

SYMPTOMS OF TETANUS

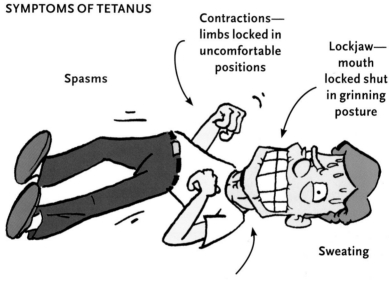

Contractions—limbs locked in uncomfortable positions

Lockjaw—mouth locked shut in grinning posture

Spasms

Sweating

Muscles in throat spasm—can't swallow, difficult to breathe

Tetanus is caused by a bacterium that likes to live in places with no oxygen, such as dirt, the intestines of animals, and poop. It is a disease associated with cuts from metal objects. This is because metal objects often come in contact with dirt, and they are sharp enough to pierce through your skin. Anything that is in contact with dirt that pierces deep into your skin can give you tetanus, including metal, glass, . . . or somebody's tooth! Animals are always sticking their noses in the dirt, either when they are eating or disobeying their humans, so tetanus is something to think about if you get badly bitten.

Animals like dirt. Tetanus in the dirt can get on animal teeth.

Don't worry, tetanus is not contagious, and not very common thanks to immunizations. Oh yeah, so *that's* why you get your shots: they protect you! You should get a tetanus shot every ten years to make sure you are safe. You should get a shot earlier if you have a bad, dirty wound. Sure, shots stink, but tetanus is worse.

Maybe adults would not like you to read this, but it is generally safe to play in dirt, especially if you've had your shots, and if you are not eating it or constantly cutting yourself. Do everyone, especially yourself, a favor by washing up afterward. But above all, make sure to wash any cuts very well.

This book also says, "Don't get into trouble."

What If You've Been Bitten by a Mammal?

1. Put pressure on the wound to control the bleeding.

2. Clean the wound as soon as possible with soap and water, or iodine if you have it. Cleansing kills rabies and other viruses. However, avoid alcohol, hydrogen peroxide, and other disinfectants since they might harm your wound.

3. A medical professional can do a good job of helping to clean your boo-boo if it is very bad by squirting and wiping away all the dirt and other gross things that might be stuck in the wound.

4. If you have a scrape, you can smear on an antibacterial ointment like Neosporin. If you have an open wound, do *not* use that antibacterial stuff, and definitely see a medical professional.

5. After everything is good and clean, cover it up with a dry, sterile (really clean) dressing, such as a Band-Aid or a piece of cloth.

6. Whatever you do, do *not* use a tourniquet! Tourniquets were used more in the olden days to stop bleeding or to stop the spread of snakebite venom. However, tourniquets can cut off the blood supply and cause even more damage! Usually, direct pressure to the wound site is the best method to control bleeding.

Armbands tied too tight are like tourniquets.

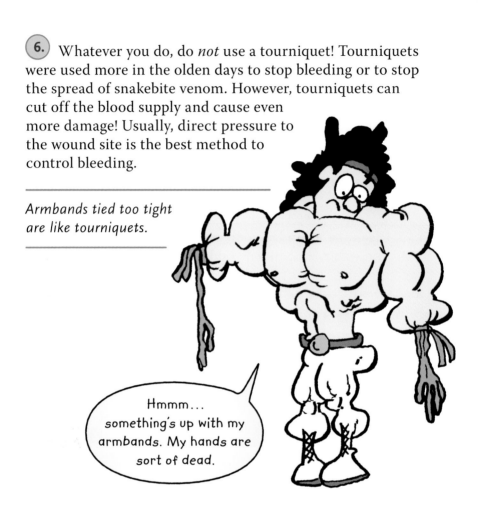

Hmmm... something's up with my armbands. My hands are sort of dead.

If you have a bad bite, go to the emergency room or to your doctor. They can do a good job cleaning your wound for you. They might also give you stitches that can help your wound heal faster and not leave as big of a scar. You may also be given a tetanus shot, and they can answer any questions about rabies.

Other Mammals

Bats

Bats are flying mammals that are helpful in many ways, especially for eating all the annoying insects that fly around. Although they may spread rabies to people, most bats do not carry the disease (probably fewer than 1 percent). When a bat has rabies, it is usually clumsy, and may not be able to fly. These infected bats are more likely to come in contact with curious people, and the disease can be spread that way.

Some people believe that bats will fly into people's hair and become entangled. However, this does not happen. This tale may have evolved from the crazy flying moves that bats do to catch bugs. Additionally, people attract a lot of bugs, so sometimes bats may dive near people in order to catch the bugs.

You do not have to worry about vampire bats in the United States. They are found in Mexico and South America. They have many interesting features, including being the only known mammal to live solely on blood. They can feed from a variety of sleeping animals. (Usually the sleeping animal doesn't even wake up!) In the wild, large livestock animals such as cows might get bitten the most. Bats bite humans much less frequently.

Bats will not fly into your hair, even if you do build a bat house on your head.

He's chasing me with a **bird**house...

Here batty batty!

Porcupines

Obviously, you shouldn't touch a porcupine. Porcupines are rodents. Big rodents. With big spines, called quills. On average, a porcupine has thirty thousand quills. Each quill has barbs, so once they get in you, they are hard to get out. Even worse, the quills are all spongy inside, so when they get wet, they expand, driving themselves further into your flesh.

Porcupines cannot "shoot" their quills like some might have you believe. The quills do come out pretty easily though, and can get stuck in anyone who offends a porcupine, so don't go touching porcupines, or insulting their mothers!

Porcupines are basically the only spiky mammals native to the United States. Hedgehogs are found in Europe, Asia, and Africa, and echidnas (spiny anteaters) are found in Australia. Some people keep hedgehogs as pets. It is OK to carefully touch these animals, since they do not have the dangerous detachable barbed quills that porcupines have. Porcupine quills are much more nasty than hedgehog or echidna spines.

21,363... 21,364... dang-nabbit! Hold still so I can count your quills!

Who had the awesome job of counting thirty thousand porcupine quills?

Skunks

It should also be obvious that you don't want to touch a skunk. In addition to their famous spray, they also like to bite! You should retreat if they start stamping their feet, put their tails up, and turn around to aim their butts in your direction!

Skunk spray is not only very smelly, it can also irritate your skin, and if it gets in your eyes, it may cause burning and temporary blindness. If you get sprayed, wash it off with whatever you have, like soap or shampoo. The best thing for getting rid of the smell might actually be diluted bleach, but ask a doctor or a smart adult how to do it, because too much bleach can burn your skin and mess you up. Other methods for getting rid of the smell include hydrogen peroxide and baking soda. Bathing in tomato juice is a popular, traditional method, but it probably just masks the skunk odor with the strong smell of tomatoes.

...And That's It!

Those are the plants and animals you have to worry about *not* touching in North America. As you can see, there are many more wonderful marvels that you *can* touch outside than you *can't* touch. If you're not sure, play it safe: just look! You can learn and enjoy a lot just by looking. Just because this book did not mention anything about resurrected saber-tooth tigers, common sense should tell you that you shouldn't touch one if you find it. Although some of the subjects in this book might sound scary or gross, knowing about them will help you be more confident about what might be dangerous and why they might be dangerous. It's still OK to freak out if some buggeroo falls on your lap . . . at least in the back of your mind you now know if it might be dangerous or not.

Don't worry, that's not a black widow!

Look! Humans!

With your new knowledge and confidence, you can be excited about discovering the natural world around you. Whether you are in a city or a forest, there are amazing and beautiful natural wonders everywhere. It is up to you to find them and keep them safe for everyone else to enjoy. Don't forget to bring along your common sense while you're out there. Stay safe, leave the natural world the way you found it, and happy exploring!

Index